Duck Soup and Swansongs

John Carey

Duck Soup and Swansongs

Acknowledgements

Five of these poems have appeared in the Canberra VC Prize Long-List Anthologies for 2014, 2015 and 2017.

Three of the poems have appeared in *The Australian Poetry Journal*.

Other poems first appeared in the following: *Blue Giraffe*; *The Canberra Times*; Central Coast Poets Anthologies 2014, 2017; *Cordite*; Spineless Wonders Microfiction collection: 'Stoned Crows and Other Australian Icons'; *Quadrant*; and *4W*.

'Balloons' won the Henry Kendall Prize for 2014.

'Brett and Arthur' was equal first in the W.B. Yeats Prize for 2014.

Dedicated to the memory of two fine poets:
John Miles and John Upton

Duck Soup and Swansongs
ISBN 978 1 76041 483 2
Copyright © text John Carey 2018

First published 2018 by
GINNINDERRA PRESS
PO Box 3461 Port Adelaide 5015 Australia
www.ginninderrapress.com.au

Contents

Duck Soup	9
Individual Agreement	11
A Catholic Boyhood (condensed)	12
Anxiety-for-a-daughter Tanka	13
Australian Poetry 1850–1945	14
Set 'em up Joe	15
Captain's Pick Haiku	16
Another Day at the Office	17
Groves of Academe	18
Seven Channels	19
Unquiet Nights of *Rage*	21
The Quick Brown Fox	22
Balloons	23
Both ends against the middle	25
Anargasm	26
Report from the circuit judge	27
Bio	28
From the Gonzo Dictionary of Literary Terms	29
Comedy Writing 101	30
Theatre	31
'Energy' at the MCA	33
Fashion Crimes	34
Brett and Arthur	35
Axel	37
he says, she says	38
Contestants	39
Financial Adviser's Report	40
Realty Spell Check	41
Flammable Agents (a treatment)	42
The Defence Sums Up	44

Dear Facebook	45
Enronics	46
Chairborne	47
At the Identity Makeover Clinic	48
Globalissima	49
Shunted Aside	50
L.R.B.	52
Crashed	54
Tokyo	55
Bagged	56
Empathy	57
Couldn't help overhearing	58
Attack of the Killer Icons	60
John C. Holmes' Bankable Asset	61
The Metrics of Eros	62
Comfort Stop	63

Swansongs — 65

Sailing for England – January 1967	67
Latitudes	69
Anniversary	70
My One and Only Love	71
Seventy reasons to say…	73
In black and white	74
Red-eye Flight	75
Speed-reading	78
From the Gonzo Film Archive	79
Darby	80
War Prints	81
A walk-through of Anish Kapoor	82
Horn	84
Branford Marsalis: Concert in New Orleans	85

Hancock–Corea Concert	86
Improvisation	87
After Bird	89
Dream Homes	90
The Third Man	92
Henry and Margaret	93
Guard Duty	95
The composer turns to the camera	96
Radical Dementia	98
Post Truth	99
Navigation	100
Panguna	102
Unravelling	103
Blurb and Counter-blurb	104

Duck Soup

Individual Agreement

Sir, about the clause in my contract
that says I will need to have a limb amputated
to enhance my visual and affective impact
for the street-corner phone-plan sales team:
I have a question.
Do I get severance pay?

A Catholic Boyhood (condensed)

So you think you've lost your Faith –
Did it have your name on it?

How many times, son, how many times?
You boastful little sod!

Nominy Dominy Hominy Deuteronomy
Give up self-abuse and astronomy.

Ten Hail Marys round the oval.

Anxiety-for-a-daughter Tanka

Cleo at age thirteen
silk-trussed like a spider's prey
spinning in the web
at bay to tweeters and trolls
dies from the bite of an app

Australian Poetry 1850–1945

When gullies were dales and creeks were brooks
there were four-figure sales for poetry books.
When the woods went bush with the swags and blackfellas
the poetry push became best-sellers
till the time was ripe for the clever blokes
and the only rich tripe was a five-star hoax.
Then depression and war seemed permanent fixtures
and most of the punters had gone to the pictures.

Set 'em up Joe

It's a bar like any other in downtown Storyville.
The animals talk and the men have speech impediments

or bad accents, like the Englishman, Irishman and Scot
or the rabbi, the priest and the mufti who drink together

when they're not walking three abreast down an unnamed street
behind three golfers who are always par for the course.

'Doctor, doctor, I think it's some sort of seizure!'
'Computer, books and papers? It's the Fraud Squad.'

'Make mine a double entendre,' says the chantoozie.
'The Senator will have the usual,' says the floozie.

Captain's Pick Haiku

the worst cabinet
since Doctor Caligari
great team be buggered

Another Day at the Office

He winds up like a pitcher on the mound
then signs a voluminous piece of paper

as if the training-wheels are still attached
to his arm   inspects the Praetorian Guard,

weeds out one whose eyebrows dance
another who looks dangerously proactive

time for a couple of executive tweets
from the lounge at the airfield   then off

to a golf course in the Emirates
with the world's largest bunker

where his own name shimmers in
mega lights that can be seen from Space.

He needs to be seen to be being something.

Groves of Academe

Finalists in the dig-off
for the Junior Archaeologist Scholarship Prize
please step forward.
Let's put all our shards on the table, shall we?
I think Rebecca has it. Good girl.
I'm sure you'll love it at Girton.
We'll tidy this away before we pour the sherry.

Seven Channels

In the credits of a crime thriller
set in the swamps of Louisiana:
'bait-buckets by Leon de Ponce
Sporting Hire of Lafayette'.

Fashions-in-the-field at the Spring Carnival:
a hat like an avian pile-up in a wind tunnel.
A colourful Racing Identity tells his partner's cleavage
the joke about the blind steeplechaser.

At the Eurovision Song Contest
the drummer in the Taras Bulba outfit
is a tap or two behind the beat
as if the others started without him.

The celebrity chef dips a manicured finger
into the crème brûlée then licks it.
She's never seen an apron outside of a threesome
with her New York agent and the French maid.

An author shows off his new dental implants
to the book club and explains himself:
'There's no bibliography. This is a self-help book.
I knew it all because the voices told me.'

A super-mum on the board of Chase Manhattan
has a twin-berth jogging pram with five-speed gears
and a Monza racing stripe. She tells her nanny she
should do something with her hair. You can have it all.

In the last reel of a heist-caper movie
a brace of body doubles sort each other out
on a loot-strewn bed in a collage of oiled limbs.
The room has windows that look out on to the unattainable.

You liked it when they showed the mother kangaroo
putting the joey to bed, then the test pattern.
It was out of your hands somehow. Now the screen
just goes black at a touch. A quiet flatlining.

Unquiet Nights of *Rage*

fauxhemian rhapsodies
psychobilly shoot-outs
with smoking banjos
motown divas warbling
and wiggling their way
into your soggy affections
knitting your insomnia
into a twitching cloak
to spread over first light
video clips over both ears
a decade of midnight to dawn
against scotophobia: fear
of the dark when groping
your way to grown-up.

The Quick Brown Fox

'The quick brown fox jumps over the lazy dog'
is a found poem of sorts in a lyric metre
fit for a Tyrolean walking song and, of course,
an efficient pangram with few repetitions
and no strain on the syntax. It is also
a popular success without peer, better known
than any line of Yeats, Auden or even the Bard.
As a child, I traced it on a slate till my fingers stiffened
and it filled the nightmares of millions of blindfolded typists.

Like many another masterpiece, it was penned by A. Nonymous
or U.N. Certain, though many names have been whispered,
from Albert the Prince Consort to Ho Chi Minh.
More likely, it was some brisk entrepreneur
of the pre-post-industrial age, like a Pitman
of shorthand fame or one of his clerks
in a false collar and an eyeshade
or perhaps there is truth in the Stalinist claim
that a Cyrillic version evolved from the struggles
of the Dactylographic Collective of downtown Tblisi.

We are learning again to shrink from Romantic excess
and see the poetic 'I' as a pre-Raphaelite self-pleasurer
or, at very least, a florid North American in a bow tie.
So let us pause to honour the authors
of 'the quick brown fox' et cetera.
Lucky it wasn't mauled by some brutalist editor
who liked to strip out articles and adjectives
till it all sounded like the name of a Navajo chief.

Balloons

The Montgolfier brothers made their first serious essay
with a billowing globe of specialty paper and taffeta
that bore in a basket their first nervous passengers:

a sheep called Climb-to-the-sky, a duck and a rooster
but although the globe with its buttoned-up panels
burst on impact like a libertine's pantalon,

the creatures emerged intact and were granted,
no doubt, a ticket of leave from the abattoir,
perhaps a royal pension. The balloons were designed

partly with a mind to overfly fortresses
and empty on the foreign jackals below
what nuisances the cash-strapped nation could afford:

baskets of oath-affirming arms, talking heads,
crushing didactic tableaux and sharpened clausulae
which might unman them and force a surrender

but worked better, in the end, against each other,
death by rhetoric and gesture, a grand guignol
theatricality with an iron-filing stench of blood

till the balloons came into their own as a
narrative device for reactionary novelists
who filled the baskets with stiff-lipped Pimpernels

powdered wigs and tear-stained décolletages
soaring to safety over the cliffs of Dover.
History as bunk, history as hissy fits in the wings

of the Comédie and the ranks of the gutter press,
history as the slap and chop in the waves of
happenstance, history as a highway with slow lanes,

passing lanes, roadblocks, bottlenecks and steaming
heaps of roadkill and with luck, surveillance from the sky
and a flyover corridor for endangered species.

Both ends against the middle

bend the structure out of shape, crack the hub
of it all, squeeze voices to a tremolo
that shatters glass, every tiny fragment
hissing through its whining bandsaw teeth.

Extending the conceit from politics to life,
neutrals are drained into inanition,
disappearing like gristle between bone-grind,
sick to death of fighting on two fronts.

Adversarial systems work only with a
guidebook of rules and a Solomonic splitting
against the grain of assertion and monomania
into two even pieces of logic. Gandhi
needed to invoke the threat of partition
seen only as a nasty hypothesis
too obviously heavy with rotten fruit.

The mentions of Solomon and Gandhi suggest
heavy reinforcement of the centre, a strength
embodied in a leader who ignored the feeble
mirage of winner-take-all triumphalism.
Irony of the inscription *INRI*
deriding the folly of the Messiah's assumed
destiny, double irony of the dividend
lying in wait in the spread of social
evolution, the soft profusion of the middle.

Anargasm

A poem that rides on its own melting
in slipstream mode to a wet nothing

is entropism, the long downtime at a
tight impasse, an indolent motor we

don't prime-heat. A soon-wilting stem
wants resetting. The lampoon idiom

wanes on a tone-timer stoplight, dim-
lit grid, phoneme waste station M on

the planet Moi, emitting no words as
a poem that rides on its own melting.

Note: each line of the poem is an anagram of the first line.

Report from the circuit judge

of the Mountain View Rhododendron and Arts Festival Poetry Competition:

A bewildering mixture of subjects and styles
much harder to judge than the sheep-dog trials.
'When he picked that one, he must have been pissed!'
you'll say, I suppose, but here's the shortlist:

a mother coping with hyperactive three-year-old quintuplets;
a recipe for gluten-free muffins in rhyming couplets;
a plea for Middle Eastern fences to be mended;
a dark and inscrutable sonnet – Highly Commended;
a concrete poem that made the line count problematical;
a II O pastiche entirely in formulas mathematical;
a page of fortune-cookie philosophy like a hash-head praying
(I know who wrote that one but I'm not saying).

To compensate for the many Dear Departeds
for the lovers too bold or too faint-hearted,
there's a Baby Boom in the entries, some even in wedlock.
A society firmly rooted down to the bedrock.
So I've given First Prize to the beleaguered mother.
I'll send this off and then I might have another.

Bio

Waldo is a third-generation Creative Writing guru
who wears his scholarship heavily and vice versa
which doesn't faze the semi-literate students
who fill his classes to the joy of the Dean and the Bursar.
He has criss-crossed the continent, shore to shining shore,
from campus to airport to another rural campus,
to conference with peers, face to face and jaw to jaw,
spreading the light to a wilderness of wheatfields and pampas.
The dad-jokes he learned in his youth were unfunny puns
removed like gallstones from the writings of Lacan and Derrida
that supplied the thrust for the last of his many runs
for Pulitzer glory. Then cuckolded by an ex-con blogger from Florida!
But he's still Prince of the Shortlist, next-to-last man standing,
too subtle for vulgar celebrity or media branding.

From the Gonzo Dictionary of Literary Terms

bugarstice

is the name of a verse form sung
by Dalmatian shepherds to their sheep
as an instrument of forced conversion
or to calm them during the rigours
of drenching and cleansing. It is a formal
measure characterised by the obligatory
caesura after the seventh syllable
that echoes the halt at nightfall
of combats against Turk or Bulgarian
or the exhaustion of sated troubadours
after their 'doux combats' with well-muscled
milkmaids. It is not to be confused
with the 'bucolic diaeresis' that resulted
from excessive consumption of fermented
sour apples, the 'Barnstaple tarantella'
of the famous passage from Chaucer.

Comedy Writing 101

Save the modifiers for your doctoral thesis.
In this class they look like a failure of nerve.
Disguise and surprise are the essence. Be a wolf
in sheep's clothing or Grandma's bedjacket, then
reverse the terms. Play silly buggers with the punter's
expectations, like the cartoon duck who surprisingly
side-steps the falling piano by stooping to pick up
a false-nickel lure, then waddles on straight into
an open manhole. Anarchy and violent pratfalls
appeal to the young male but for the nursing-home
performance, try something gentler. Though choosing
material to second-guess the expected audience
often comes unstuck. As well it should. That's comedy.
Young Mr Elton is fidgeting. He's easily bored. Good.
Better show your scripts to him first. I'll be finishing
the crossword in my office. Reconvene at 14.00.

Theatre

In Zuckmayer's *The Captain of Köpenick*, an ex-general,
now Kommandant of a Prussian prison, has a company of
toothless old lags riding brooms up a ramp to re-enact
a famous cavalry charge: 'Ah, my brave lads !'
drools the ancient general, 'what a fine body of men!'

In a Brendan Behan play, a stage direction:
a nun in full habit shuffles on to the scene and in one
swift movement, removes the habit to reveal
a man in a shabby suit who informs the audience:
'I'm a secret policeman and I don't care who knows it!'

From Joe Orton: a young expectant mother
without benefit of wedlock, is counselled by a woman
social worker of sinister gentility and born-again smugness:
'Now don't get me wrong. There is no more beautiful sight
than two young married people making love.'

From Howard Barker, a scene set in the vault
of the newly established Bank of England: a dissipated
Charles II, a louche mistress, a wide-boy cockney courtier
and the sudden irruption of a furious Yorkshire merchant:
'Piece of paper be buggered! I want to see my money, I want to touch it!'

Howard Barker again. A conference in the Kremlin:
Churchill, Stalin, a nervous foul-mouthed interpreter
and a bewildered Scottish comedian. (Stalin has been
misinformed that Churchill loves Scottish comedians.)
'I can't fucking translate that! This bastard will kill us all !'

An Oz sample? Not easy. Deadpan lines. Have to be there.
From Williamson: the middle-aged son tells his father that
he has just left his wife for his mistress. That night, the old dad
catches him in flagrante on the sofa with yet another woman,
half his age. The patriarch shakes his head: 'Just not good enough, son.'

'Energy' at the MCA

The young lady facilitator ushers us in
to the soundproof anechoic chamber
and closes the door 'For the full experience…
just push it open if you've had enough…'
We wait. At ankle level there is light
from white patterns on the floor that
look like triangular teeth, otherwise
pitch black, as if we are in the maw
of a great white shark. In the background
is the faintest monotonic hum like the
soundtrack of your whole life speeding
past you. The door finally eases open
and the girl asks 'How was it?'
'Do other couples get up to mischief here?'
She freezes. 'You don't mean to say…'
'It was on our bucket list.'

Fashion Crimes

A model in concubine belt and fetish harness
formally gagged with a black butterfly.
Another whose young cosseted skin will never

look any better, is tagged with an ugly tattoo
the length of her arm. Repurposed fabrics,
repurposed clichés, the playful motifs

of cathouse and jailhouse chic. *Un succès
de vandale* for the young designer who does it
because he can, invested with the power

of societal life and death. Not a man
you would take home to meet your grandma.
She would strangle him with a blue stocking.

Brett and Arthur

Whiteley in the Rimbaud museum at Charleville,
naked, with a photo of the poet covering his face,
something of a larrikin touch to the homage,
good-humoured worlds away from the shit-on-God graffito
that Arthur would daub on walls around the drab town
he had to boomerang back to when he ran out of cash.

Nothing surprising at first in the lure of Rimbaud:
the flammable property of poetry, Art as an all-up bet,
ambitions beyond the station of any art or craft,
the siren song of transgression, absinthe and hashish
as a leg up to climb out of yourself into something
that would see the big picture, be the big picture.

In his own portrait of Rimbaud, Whiteley doesn't stray far
from the only clear photograph of the young poet
and fills most of the canvas with a rendering
of emanations from the poet's brain. Partial inventory:
rounded hillocks and boulders, a white staircase
curving and tapering back into yellow sand, in the distance,

a rearing shark with the hint of a quivering buttock,
a mouth like a hammerhead vulva and something
that looks like the island of Doctor Moreau. Brett's
copied-out passages from Rimbaud might suggest only
a cursory reading but the details of the picture
point to a strong grasp of motifs and sources.

I have seldom found the surrealist mode disturbing
where the psyche seems to reach out to the ambient world.
There is often a lush efflorescence in the works,
more fluid and dynamic than the clinging shapes,
the stalled moves and furred textures of nightmare. Here,
there's a South Seas sunniness that undoes Arthur's ferocity.

For the better, perhaps. And Whiteley's other representation
of Arthur? The sculpture of two huge matches, one live, one dead?
I must have blinked and missed the flare in between. Or I needed
warmth in my life, not a conflagration. A lost weekend
in Hell was season enough and illumination best dammed
and released in a steady trickle of lucidity.

Brett asked the question about Van Gogh: 'Is Art worth a life?'
The answer for me is 'no' if it didn't need to be. So what
do you do when you're not delirious? Arthur:
'I set myself up as an exemplary burnt-out case
and mind a shop in a hellhole in Africa.' Brett:
'I roll down my sleeves and get on with the job.'

Axel

I found the famous Melbourne underground artist, Axel
'Chocka' Blok, nailing stray cats
to the cathedral door. 'I'm completing my thesis,' he
explained. 'What course is that?'
I asked and should have known better. 'The entrée,' he said.
We recorded the interview back
at his place, a three-storey lifestyle apartment made over from a
heritage incinerator.
I started with a leading question: 'How would you define
outlaw art?'
'I don't need to,' he said, 'there's always blokes like you who'll
do it for me.'
'Well, let me put it more simply,' I suggested. 'When you've
tested the limits of transgression
and pushed the envelope inside out, what will you find on the
other side of the funhouse mirror?'
'Put simply,' he said, 'my exhibitions are curated by the Crown
Prosecutor. I think I might
nail you to the door of the art gallery.'
'I'll want a contract,' I demurred. 'Will I be a statement, a
happening or a valuable artefact?
There's a fee scale.'
'You'll be an exhibit,' said Axel. 'Exhibit A: "The Hand That
Feeds Me". Exhibits have no
rights. I do gratuitous crimes. Brace yourself.'

he says, she says

When I downsized to a Girl Friday with district views
I hid the boat and the time-share condo offshore
told the kids it was nice knowing them which was untrue:
I didn't and it wasn't. Their mother took to my shirts
with a pair of scissors then I used them on her credit cards.
When I'd first mentioned key-swapping, she swapped hers
for a high C that shattered crystal. 'I loved you once,'
she said, 'when you seemed edgy and dangerous but now…'
I pleaded guilty to suspend her sentence that wasn't
going anywhere I wanted to be, which was somewhere
else. 'Remember the good times for both of us,'
I said, closing the door gently to keep it civilised.
'Forty is the new twenty,' I said to myself, 'the old one
was rubbish.' I'm forty-seven but I like round numbers.

Contestants

The ones we pick are close to the edge at the start,
prone to hysteria and fits of temper. They know
what to expect: sleep deprivation, sudden shifts
in the filming schedule, creative editing
that makes them look like dickheads (which they are),
nasty tweets from the sick end of the spectrum
or sent by us just to hurry things along.

Then we drum them out, one by one, a ceremony
based on a scene from the film of the Dreyfus
Affair. The best way to deflate the self-esteem
of a drama queen is total humiliation. My son
calls me a monster, says that the whole show
is like a cruel parody of a detention centre, or worse,
with the inmates made to kill and bury each other.

Sense of proportion, my son! I have to point out
that we have a counsellor and a team of lawyers
to deal with flip-outs and breaches of contract.
The real monsters are the True Believers.
Me, I'm a cynical manipulator of people
who can't cope without one. I only do it for
money and the market has a built-in sunset

clause: the viewers get sick of it and we move on.
Next year I might be mowing lawns or have to produce
a nice lost dog segment for the get-in-touch-with-your-
better-self bracket before Late News and Weather.
You'll like that. It's to pay your school fees and your
mother's shopping therapy and customised diet plan.
So shut up and be proud of me. People forget.

Financial Adviser's Report

The company has a website of course.
In fact, it is a website pure and simple
with a listing on the Bucharest Bourse
to try to put a backside on the pimple.
There's a fleet of trucks from various lines
for sundry goods to fall off the back of
and escort cuties dressed up to the nines
booking gigs from a boarding house in Cracow.

The CEO is a paintball sniper
and MBA in powerpoint presentations,
tucking dodgers under your windscreen wiper
and starting phone calls with 'congratulations!'
Unless your greed for profit is obsessive,
note that the risk assessment reads 'aggressive'.

Realty Spell Check

a new release of rehabilitated badland
near the Olganga Mine in the Panhandle

for first home buyers and their soulmates
to plough the acres of schist and dolomite

for a maiden crop of vig and carspace
district views and vibrant absentia

by the bindii-boxes the pitched doof
the woof of outhouse explosions

a dreaming of serial jackpots
and beads of frost on a glass eye

suit investors or smart casual likewise
white-shoe self-starters and clean last-chancers

opportunity puts the boot in so make me an offer
gazump yourself and I'm sure to go one better

Flammable Agents (a treatment)

begins with a mutual paint-stripping stare.
Friend or foe or both? What they have in common
is quarryhood, huntedness, the chance of being locked together
in a crime-scene, one innocent victim at least, but if so, which?
A murder attempt on them in the first reel and a narrow escape.
Then they couple grimly like pedalling an exercise bike.

A post-coital spat and she tells him, 'On your bike!
And I don't mean me!' But too late. A footstep on the stair
outside. A wheezing Pizza delivery boy? On the fire escape?
A chase over rooftops and across Wandsworth Common
where they run slow-motion through flower beds, during which
they shake the fat hitman, hide and collapse together.

The dangerous foreplay is why they come together
every time in forty seconds with an angry-sounding bi-
cornous groan. One at least is faking but we can't tell which.
Her I suppose. He doesn't really rate as a stayer.
We switch to a debate on home security in the Commons.
Budget cuts everywhere. Even the spooks won't escape.

Serious issues here. No helter-skelter escape
from plausibility without a struggle. The plot strands mesh together
with every hair out of place. Spooks and bonkers will make common
cause: defence of Freedom and cheap outsourcing with bi-
cameral applause. Switch to the hitman with the thousand-yard stare
and a bead on the target pair. He'll hit the one on top but we can't guess which.

The killer's with a rogue outfit but we don't know which
or whether he's freelancing but there's no escape
for the trysting co-stars surely. Their rolling stair-
way to heaven is soon to be interruptus. He might get both together
with a single shot. Then we spot a man with a baguette on a pre-war bike.
The loaf spits fire and he doesn't miss. Dei ex machina all have this in common.

The lovers and the plot are fogbound in a common
quandary: loose ends to trail or tie, it's even money which
but there's always the sequel. They climb on his Harley bike
to ride off to witness protection as a bogus couple, so no escape
from each other. Will they manage to stick together?
In sweaty leathers, probably. Like Spencer and Kate, Ginger and Fred Astaire.

Escape from reality as trenchcoat & raincoat, poke & dagger, a common
coupling of genres that belong together, like apples and pears. Up to you which
of the modes rides the sidecar and which steers the bike.

The Defence Sums Up

He couldn't have used his car. They were fixing the steering.
The mysterious red traces turned out to be herring.
So here's a man who entertained thoughts of murder?
The complete reverse is true. Componite verba.
The prosecution case is a catalogue of failure.
The suspicious van was the 7 News make-up trailer.
The Crown's star witness, the aptly named Miss Farrago,
under pressure, shifted and rolled like an unsecured cargo.
On the night in question, an unshakable alibi:
my client met with the Prime Minister. Would he lie ?
Unexplained sightings in bizarre places, juicy snippets
of gossip? Elementary. My client is a known triplet.
And the empty grave was disturbed from the inside out.
Would you say that constitutes reasonable doubt?

Dear Facebook

I now have a hundred and twenty-two imaginary friends
who all look like Justin Bieber except for the boys.
My mother sets place-mats out for them and imaginary chairs,
serves them pink lemonades with bonsai umbrellas
and asks them what their fathers do when they're not absconding.
She's a patronising bitch, my mother, as I never
stop telling her in the nicest possible way.
She who dropped me off at a holiday boot camp
for the gifted and lonely and didn't pick me up
till the thaw hit Thredbo in September. Last visit,
I asked my dad if I could have an imaginary puppy.
'You are an imaginary puppy,' he said. 'Ask your mother.'

Enronics

There's a dissenting voice among the auditors:
'Front-end loaded earnings that bias the denominator
in the PE ratio and a timing disconnect between
the projects' cash and earnings effects…
this is a whole shit-load of dysfunctionality.'
'So we proactively manage our balance sheet
to achieve target rating. So what? This man
is not an effective advocate of the story.
His bosses need a strong message as to how
viscerally senior management feel about
this sort of negativity. Cut him off at the knees!'
'Well, I dealt with that!' the CEO tells himself,
as he drafts his next billion-dollar adventure.
'This looks like déjà vu all over again!'

Chairborne

The Treasurer sifts and sorts
his cherry-picked data, rorts

the stats, projections and parameters,
poses at his desk for the news cameras

then does his sums, the only part of the job
he studied for: how much change from the two bob

his mum gave him to go to the corner shop,
how many years take his pension to the top

scale before he quits. Pity the rates are pegged
to those of the civil service, the dregs

left over from the binges of the other team
before they were tipped from office, who seem

to love answering questions you don't ask
and fail to understand that the real task

is selling the budget, not shaping it.
Sell punters a pup and it takes two years to wake up to it.

At the Identity Makeover Clinic

my spin doctor has put me on a course
of Transcendental Social Mediation.
'Any side-effects, doctor?'
'At worst, after the session, you may
feel a little confused and bland
and your combative edge
will slip back into its sheath
but it'll come back sharper
than ever for the R&R.' So I let
my Facebook followers lead me
where they may and tell myself:
'I am not a controlling person
any more than a goose in the middle
of the squadron decides if the flock
will wheel left or right. I am
a consultative centrist through
and through.' Thank you, doctor,
I'm half in love with you already,
a natural transference, I believe,
as from account to account and
one budget to the next. A propos,
your bill is outrageous and would
make my old self unmanageably
angry and if this doesn't work
I'll hold you accountable. OK
I'll make another appointment.

Globalissima

We have all, it seems, put our hands up
to be offshored into the Tourist Park
of Southern Europe with pocketfuls
of heavy Ozdolls. We are encapsulated
in a metal container, like summaries
of something more expansive. As we wait
for long minutes in the exit aisles,
I can't lace up my shoes. Thrombosis?
Elephantiasis? A patina of footsmell
gone thick and solid?
                      In the hub of town
we promenade in a fairytale village
of Irish pubs with names like Flannerie's
or Dorsal Finn McCool, run by Romanian
ex-rugby-players and screening English
Premier League from dusk till dawn.
By midnight I am asking the big questions:
How many Ozdolls to the Euro ?
How many sheets to the wind ?
How long is a piece of string bikini ?

Shunted Aside

I'm the only old duffer in the carriage,
in the company of the post-me generations,
the unknown quantities. It seems

they have riffled the pages of angst
and anomie, put them back in the rack
then walked away with only a jittery disquiet

and a taste for divertissement,
excitements as fragile as balloons
drifting in a forest of kittens.

But the fine motor skills in their slim
fingers put me to shame, I who only learned
to tie a fish-hook at the tenth attempt.

I watch them negotiate the ticket scan
at the exit gate, their free hands still
texting or tweeting with a desperate

intensity to hold off the hypnotic
snake-stare of an inner life. Each to the other,
we are as shallow as touchscreens

with sequences to be solved with a quick
flick, like propping prone photos up
to the vertical. I feel deleted.

O brilliant kids, frisk with your iPods
but don't take the traffic lights as a personal
rejection. Red means red, no means no,

a bus is still a bus, so don't step
under it sending a last text to God:
'I'm entitled to something better.'

L.R.B.

An older friend has made me the gift
of a subscription to the *London Review of Books*
better by far in keeping dementia at bay
than Sudoku or the Friday cryptic crossword.
It works for him. He still writes as well as ever.

I seize on a heading: 'Man-Eating Philosophers'
(Heidegger, Heidegger burning bright…?) and think
of the Monty Python World Cup of Philosophy,
a match-up between Greece and Germany: 'a slow
dribble by Kant, a scything tackle from Plato. Penalty!'

I find some items for my Compendium
of Unspeakable Verbs (leaving out my own coinages
which I've worn in like new shoes). 'Apotheosise'
is a bit elephantiasised, having outgrown its concept
like a belly thrown over the pants you wore for your wedding.

'Synergise', cornered by the puff doctors, is forever
foutu. 'Metastasise' is best left to the doctor-doctors.
'Googled' and 'You-Tubed' must be OK since I've used them
myself. 'A tendriling [sic] social network' is icky enough
but discredit is given to the author who's being worked over.

Some lexical challenges: 'Bildungsroman'
I know from my Dictionary of Literary Terms
and feel smug about it. Herr Uber-Nerd
and Herr Cyber-Macher remind me of a lovely
couple we met once in an Internet café.

There are words and phrases I like with a subtext in mind:
each one has 'steal it!' written all under it. 'Ideolect'
and 'semantic clumps' may still have legs but
'disintegrated in a shower of sparkling pixel flakes'
is too distinctively fine to be easily deniable.

There are images that I need a clearer picture
of in my mind, perhaps with some dots to join.
But 'the putatively anthropophagic husband and wife'
and the 'auto-cannibalistic tea parties'
are frames from a graphic novel I don't want to read.

Then I find a phrase that could trigger
a whole Bildungsroman about one of the schools
I once taught at. 'The philosophe's pedagogical
fuck-buddies', a roman à clef that ex-colleagues
and a team of lawyers would be eager to see.

A final bon mot from Will Self, the reviewer:
'if actors are to play intellectuals, they need
mind-doubles for the risky theorising scenes'.
Thanks to Will whom I've hommaged shamelessly
and to the author of *Consumed*, David Cronenberg.

Crashed

I wake up in a Japanese capsule hotel
wearing a toe tag. It's all about turnover.
Sleep in late and you're dead. After a night embrace
of the Asian Century, giving the Suntory
a cruel larruping, I am stalked by one of those
ghost stories that smother you like a stifled yawn.
No wallet, no watch, no shoelaces. Shoelaces?
Mixed messages here. What harm could I do myself?
No room to swing a cat. Capsules as skinny
as layers of lasagne. Big-nosed Westerners
have to be wrestled sideways before being slid out
by a concierge in a speckled lab coat.
My body is goosebumped like a ping-pong paddle.
My hair is stiff with frost. Watch my lips move. Please.

Tokyo

It makes every other city I've seen
seem understated. How would it all
not topple from its own weight? By doing small
in a forest of big, the two-man boutique police

stations spaced at short intervals, the bonsai
fire engines, the compact bathrooms that offer
a full hygienic experience sat on your backside
with your knees almost touching your forehead.

More important still is a gentle straitjacketing
of the ego, assertiveness trimmed to fit a concept
of civic good manners. I saw a line of protesters
at a railway station, their disquiet never ratcheted

up to public anger, a 'NO' of the same modest size
on every placard, occupying a thin slice of kerbside.
In a land of low-key manifestations of fervour,
It's patience that can have the power to frighten.

Bagged

The battered Toyota starts to zigzag across the sand
like a cockroach hearing a newspaper slowly rolled
into a club. If it could somehow climb up a crosshair
and swing itself out of the kill zone…the odds
on SportsBet point to a zap, odds about when not if.
Paf ! and the bad-day emoticons inside the vehicle
are vaporised to a pink mist. The camera's point
of view spells 'you' with your finger on the button.
Doubts and verifications belong to the back story
settled before the game started as they had to be
or there wouldn't be a game, would there? Simple
logic. If the abolished dead were anything else
but enemy combatants, it would be unthinkable.
If you didn't trust us, you wouldn't be watching.

Empathy

He might be an auctioneer he speaks so fast
to a mobile phone no doubt, white cords
trailing from his ears like a drip feed,
his hand flicking from side to side as if dealing
blackjack at the Casino. He cuts off debate
with a crisp 'whatever' and a karate chop
with his right hand like Robespierre having
the last word then sashays off the kerb

into the path of a bus, bounces off bruised and
shaken but soon hits the button for a new call.
I have just failed to witness a first-world calamity
that puts your empathy to the stretch and I recall
the words of an old Trot of my acquaintance who
dismissed the 'incident' at the World Trade Centre
as 'the death of a few stockbrokers' and left me
speechless. Is this the compassion underload

you feel when hearing the story of a bushwalker
killed by a block of frozen toilet waste
fallen from a passing aircraft or homicidal
beach buggies on Fire Island? Nothing but
a half-cocked snigger tipped with Schadenfreude
as you wait for the urban myth with your name on it
to wrap you into a stuttering microfiction
and rocket you off into cyberspace.

Couldn't help overhearing

'I mean, like, it's your property
so I thought, oh my god…'
a scrap of metadata caught on the wing
brayed into a pink mobile phone

by a no-nonsense woman on a railway platform
upping the decibels as if she had a bad line
which she did, then a worse line then another,
the message migrating to a monster warehouse

in a bald industrial estate to be picked
over and decrypted by spooks who squeeze
her 'oh my god' into a translation:
'I was awed…embarrassed…shamefaced…

disgusted…mortified et cetera' before they settle
on 'at a loss for words' then try to guess
a context: a lessee explaining unspecified
damage to her landlord? A wife finding

a pair of strange knickers in the glovebox
of the car? Then the theories take
a turn for the weird. The important thing
is that nothing is unimportant, even at

sixty-seven degrees of separation
and ambiguity from the seminal call,
a suspected terrorist sending his brother
a birthday text of curious phrasing, an odd

word resembling the first name of the braying
lady. Coincidence? Not what they're paid for.
She is now the hundred-thousandth name
on the watch list, a milestone that wins her

a set of steak knives? Maybe not.
Anything she likes from the second shelf
of soft toys, the ones that say: 'that's nice'
and roll over when you rub their bellies.

The system powers on at 2.5 teraflops
with an unknown number of bellyflops.
It sorts out stuff-ups at the speed of a thick
attorney-general who doesn't give a toss.

Nothing to fear with your mouth shut
and your fingers in splints. Only
an X-ray plate with a spreading shadow
that will open its wings inside you.

Attack of the Killer Icons

Imagine being hit in mid-snorkel by a speeding truck with teeth…the nine lives of funnel-webs fifteen hours on the bottom of a swimming pool or fifty minutes in a clothes dryer clinging to a pair of smouldering knickers…a King Brown warming his long spine and bringing his root-canals to the boil on the bonnet of your limousine…old man croc barrelling through a sewer-grate spitting bones and backpacks…a slow smile for the Japanese honeymooners and a slow voice from Longreach via Alabama:
'Have a good one, do ya heah? Ay!'
Crick go the sheilas, boys, crick crick crick…cicadas swelling into the soundtrack as the sniffer dogs paw at the ground–

In despair, you cling to a happy thought like a lifebuoy…but in the midst of life, there is a rusty stove chained to your leg.

John C. Holmes' Bankable Asset*

At first anguiform and ominous as any python to a
trapped mouse, when digitally enhanced,
it hardened to a punishing shillelagh. In photos accessible to
the softer-core magazines, it was a towel rack fit to balance
Gargantua's beach towel and bathers besides, bigger and sillier
than Texas. I wouldn't have minded half his luck and would
have settled for thirty per cent, but the thought of spending
my life as a dog, forever fainting from loss of blood to the
brain and being wagged by an enormous tail – exhibit A for a
Martian theory of human evolution.

His Wikipedia bio has a life off screen more two-
dimensional than he showed to the camera, the downhill
trajectory an abject lesson to gladden the hearts of the
religious Right:
drugs, suspicion of murder, unprotected sex when he knew
he was HIV positive, death from AIDS.
I imagine a last scene that couldn't have happened: his body
lying in state for a queue of mourners,
leather vest, string-tie, ten-gallon hat and confederate flag,
hat big enough to cover his face, flag
at half-mast.

* John C. Holmes was a porn star, spectacularly well equipped for his line of work.

The Metrics of Eros

The moves can be intricate but don't have to be,
the mutual endowments not crucial. It's not
the Olympics with margins and personal bests.

If it's good enough for both of you most of the time,
you've won. If you don't watch the wrong films
or dance to a social media self-wrap number

where my orgasm is better than yours
or my choices expand exponentially
while yours are stuck in the best you can do.

It's not about power or consumer envy,
framing the rules so you finish on top,
hollow victories won at the point of a gun.

I read a French novel once where the emotional
context was so nuanced and the voltage kept
so low that finally when there was a faint

hint of a spark and a whispered, sidelong
mention of '*petites satisfactions nocturnes*'
the words seemed to boom like a cannon.

Comfort Stop

Friedensreich Hundertwasser
is a name that comes not trippingly
off a Maori or pakeha tongue
yet he was the pride of Kawakawa
and a Living Treasure of New Zealand,
an internationally known ecologist
and architect and above all,
in the popular mind, the Klimt of the khazi,
creator of the world's most charming
and beautiful toilet block,
a chef d'oeuvre of Loo Art Deco,
columns and arches that marry
a Mad King Ludwig kitsch
to the frosty decadence
of Viennese orientalism,
plus a nod to the Alice in Wonderland
embrace of a crazy-paved world.
There's also a sense of the Antipodean
flair for ad hoc improvisation,
unlikely local materials that come to hand,
the co-option of workers given a chance
to exercise their crafts and tours de main.

It's a tourist hub, approached by a tiptoed
sword-dance through flailing selfie sticks.
The trompe l'oeil windows, necessarily opaque,
are bottles in pastel shades like lime, puce
and lavender. The asymmetrical tiles evoke the slow,
deliberation of the builder of a drystone wall
but the symphony of shapes and colours
has all the sophistication of a painter's practised eye
that takes the artless layman's breath away.

In the off-season, it must be a focus
for the locals, a comfort and convenience
stop for polite gossip, hard to conceive of
the other kind in such an ambience.
Imagine a Clochemerle pissoir sunny side up:
no sinister rendezvous, no political
cabals or vicious rumours. The spiritual
force of Hundertwasser lingers still.

Swansongs

Sailing for England – January 1967

I got plenty of advice before I left, none of it useful.
From a disenchanted and slightly sinister ex-tutor:

'There's a trip to England in every *News of the World*:
earnest vicars servicing their flock
MI5 cruising Soho in twinset and pearls
the Lord Privy Seal in an off-the-shoulder frock…'

From a mythomaniac old uni mate, drunk as usual:

'Say hello from me to Bazza McKenzie.
We went out one night in Carlton for a wee drink.
That's how I invented the term "laconic frenzy"
when he cleared the drip-tray and drank the purple ink.'

I explained to my staid, Lancashire-born Uncle Albert,

'I'm not thinking of pigeon-racing in Wigan
when you ask me if I'm looking for my roots.
Maybe Mary Quant and a catwalk full of twiggies
in mini military coats and thigh-high boots.'

Dad and Mum were last to leave the boat for the shore,
a bit teary (Mum) and quietly concerned (Dad).
I didn't help much. The only picture I could draw
of my future was vague but none the less grandiose
for that. The gist of it was that I wouldn't be back soon.

Who didn't come to see me off? There were two
who might've been there logistically, but weren't.
Which doesn't stop me seeing them in my mind's eye:
Gough with a farewell speech: 'Men and Women
of Australia. For years, the best of you have gone away.
In my humble opinion, if I ever had one,
it's time we gave you a reason to stay.'

And then he was waving…waving   (refrain)
like a silk robe in a Southerly gale
and then he was waving…waving
like a man whose strength will never fail…

Harold Holt, dapper in his best bag-o-fruit,
with a Brylcreemed baby seal on his head:
'You should be doing jungle training at Kokoda
but never mind. I'll be waiting when you come back.'

And then he was waving…waving…
'you'll live to fight another day'
and then he was waving…waving…
and in a blink he was swept away…

And all the rest of them: Normie Rowe, Dougie Walters
Nat Young, the stockmen from Wave Hill, young
Charles up from Timbertop: 'Say hello to Mummy…'

When you do, she'll be waving…waving…
for another fifty years
and there I was waving…waving…
through the streamers and the tears…

Latitudes

Rimbaud in Paris, reeking
of anisette and slept-in tatters ,
makes sheep's eyes at his betters,
wolf's eyes at his peers.

Malcolm Lowry in Mexico,
eyes like lava, nose erupting,
smells of sulphur, cactus and lemon,
a talent that feeds on its own combustion.

Faulkner, a steadier role-model,
not on the jigger scale but socially.
He doesn't get out much, probably
can't make it to the door.

Auden in New York, a cannier
pact with the devil, carousing at night
but never on an empty stomach,
then stoked on uppers, working all day.

Such were my thoughts when in 1968
in Marseille, I was helped up off the floor
by a regal Ghanaian prostitute and told that I
was a disgrace to the English-speaking community.

Anniversary

We could renew our vows
in bucking currents of air,
skydiving with the Special Forces chaplain,
blog our most intimate conjugations
for a million gawping screen-jockeys,
make the length and breadth of our celebrations
the last word in managed events
or I could give you a simple bunch of flowers
(it would be the first time)
we could go dancing
(it would be the second time with real intent)
and we could go on meeting like this
in the usual place, always with the best table,
watch the children, forever infants,
do every cute thing on cue
then sleep for hours in their pram.
Then the gypsy violinist would say,
'This one's on me.'
and stuff banknotes in your garter belt
and when the staff and the other diners
had melted away into the wings
you could say 'Just hold me'
and this time I would.

My One and Only Love

A show tune from another era
in the rich caramel voice of Johnny Hartman
backed by the John Coltrane quartet.
There must be a pre-retro on the flipside
of post-modern, a lack of knowingness
in the words 'sweet surrender', no sense
of a social or sexist agenda, a retreat
to the delicate language of Ronsard,
an urgent need, carefully dressed for dinner.

For all its urbanity,
this is a heat of the moment song,
all first-night nerves, devouring flames
and possession which is nine-tenths
of the law of diminishing returns,
a love too hot not to cool down
with a foretaste of ashes in the mouth.

It's not a passion that keeps its store
of urgency when the curtain drops
and the world closes in, a love that survives
the loss or chronic illness of a child,
the claims of a job you hate but can't do without,
those personal dreams you feel you bargained away,
a sense that the sum of you was more than the parts
until it wasn't.

A love song that starts where this one finishes
belongs in an a cappella studio
a dozen Metro stations from Tin Pan Alley.
However much we are one flesh
and of a single mind, there is space
somewhere in our overlapping circles
for a jealously guarded store of privacy,
infantile fantasies and undiscovered shame
and the little chorus line of selves that live
in the minds of those who have known us
separately.

Respecting the boundaries, taking off shoes
in the temple precinct, dressing for dinner.
That's how we secure the perimeters
of our sweet surrender. Our one and only us.

Seventy reasons to say…

It's degree zero in terms of frippery
no make-up   a little tousled from sleep
in improvised summer night attire

a bit of everything and not much of anything
no longer young though you still look much better
than I deserve and you wake well   a touch

languid but alert with a sparkle in the eye
so I don't even check the clock to see if I'm missing
the round-up of results from the Premier League

and we reach for each other less urgently perhaps
than once (not that it was ever desperate in a way
that masks uncertainty or insecurity) but

unambiguously because we know where we're going
old enough to know better if it got any better which
it maybe won't   then I hum the Beatles' 'When I'm

64' mentally changing a digit and wonder why
such bright young men in full swing through
a stellar career were so lacking in ambition.

In black and white

(after Jacques Roubaud)

Death
as absence
and total presence
a dragging anchor
on the lives of the living
In a bare room hour after hour
from dimness to dazzle
to crawling shadow
images of your beautiful young wife
her photographs of herself
standing at the window
naked on the floor of the same bare room
sometimes a vague and delicate
visitant from an earlier
superimposed picture
her professional life   her life tout court
drifting in a play
of slanting sunlight and toxic
currents of silver nitrate
her sense of herself
in black and white
and brumous wisps of grey
a fly in a web of non-being
Snap Lock Clasp
An embrace and a shutting-out
A click of the switch
Snap out of it   back into it
On both sides of the curtain
this adamantine
dark.

Red-eye Flight

A numbing twelve-hour flight and at the end of it
my first scheduled appointment, a funeral:
a friend from an earlier life, seen a few months ago
on a brief visit. She stayed for just a week,
long enough to make a new nest for herself
in the bric-a-brac of my habits and attachments.
There was no physical intimacy, just a quiet
stripping back to an almost blank page
under all the smudges and erasures.
Then she flew away to die in another hemisphere.

Albertine was the French assistant of a college
in Bristol. I saw her in the downtime between classes
reading a tattered paperback with rhythmic nods
of her head, like a jazz buff pecking at the off-beat.
It was a Malraux novel, a favourite of mine. I asked
what she thought of the story of the tram conductor,
who cares nothing for politics, taken for a combatant
by the Falangists because of the strap mark on his shirt.
As he faces the firing-squad, he makes a fist and shouts:
'Venceremos!' Was this a lesson in how to die or how
to live or just an arm of honour for the apostles of death?

I remember us drifting arm in arm from a party,
discussing the rift between Sartre and Merleau-Ponty.
We took our foreplay seriously in those days.
At year's end, Albertine was off to Algeria
to join her father, a medical coopérant with a
UN team. As the time grew closer we began
to bicker like children past their bedtime.
My last words to her were the tired formula:
'Soigne-toi.' Look after yourself. There was
a brittleness about her at the time and where
she was going wasn't the safest place in the world.

No contact for thirty years except by mail. I try
to imagine a different trajectory for my life
that I seem to have watched glide past like a
passenger in a train with his back to the engine.
A ten-year relationship that stuttered to a stop
for which I was found guilty in my emotional
absentia. Some weekend excursions to bohemia.
A few hare-brained adventures that cost me
less than I deserved. Albertine once did a burlesque
reading of my palm. Her verdict: 'A wistful
viciousness that will never amount to much.'

The in-flight movie is a slow comedy
with space to doze between the semaphoring of a joke
and its forced landing. Even the shallowest dream
can stop bad faith in its tracks: I seem to see
the celebrity faces from the picture clues
of the giant crossword turn into figures from a
book on marine biology: sea urchins, stingers,
Medusae. And among them the face of Albertine
fresh from the shower, her hair in wet strings,
her eyes enormous, searching me out.
Was her absence always to be the last word?

In the next fitful sleep, my unconscious has rushed
ahead to beat me to the funeral. We hear the eulogy
rolled out: a life of scholarship and public service.
I meet Albertine's daughter and a grand-daughter
aged ten. The dark eyes and metaphysical emphasis
of her grandmother. She asks me, 'Who are you?'

Speed-reading

Social consolidation: two Estates only,
the Third and the Gated, the latter shifting transparency
to the former who are hacked then monetised.
The Fourth Estate? Dumbed down and out of the game.
Social Media, the new Estate without number,
jostle for space in the blender, a community
of tosh and body-parts. High Retro has gone
from elite to preterite in a blink, the dawning
of a new Ark Age, where most of us miss the boat
and talk underwater for fifteen seconds,
invoking a Great Helmsman to ensure a future
already ensured and bearing down on us.
From the stockade on the hill, 360 degrees
of water views and cocktails on the patio.
Skol. Another vodka and Red Bull and be damned!

From the Gonzo Film Archive

US Military Intelligence in full evolution
from exploding cigars and toxic wetsuits
designed for Fidel to staring at goats

disarmingly till their horns drop off
or wrapping themselves in a full-body bubble
of invisibility by flexing the toned muscles

of the psyche, the way a three-year-old plays
hide-and-seek by standing in the middle
of a paddock with his eyes shut (hiding)

or open instead of counting to fifty (seeking).
The liaison officer from Noosa suggests that
none of this would work on brush turkeys

who just keep coming down the aisle of
the supermarket making for the popcorn.
There are background flashes of J. Edgar Hoover

in a tutu, Patton in his invisible bubble of
competence, Colin Powell covering his eyes
so George W. won't find him and ask him

to please explain. From slapstick to Zen and back
in a pulsating diorama. I feel like a fly on the wall,
the prototype with the tiny camera, shooting sparks.

Darby

The ugliest dog I've ever seen
is a bulldog cross or cross bulldog
that looks like a Tasmanian Devil
cast into a Gadarene swine.
Old Joe, his owner, tells me he answers
to 'Darby', after a jockey of days past,
because he's short, cranky and a bit
crooked. Darby and Joe. Cute.
The concept, that is, not the physiognomy
of dog or owner. Love has strange
pathways, each marked with its own special
scent. Old dog, old owner, their life clocks
synchronised, limping to the same appointment,
like hollowed-out shapes won from volcanic mud.

War Prints

(of Otto Dix, 1914–19)

Stylised in some measure
the way we disguise a nightmare
to keep it at a distance
or it disguises itself
to catch us unawares
but real enough to shake us –
the shattered faces, eyes that have seen
what no one was meant to see,
living bodies larval and opalescent
like those that clean up the dead.
After all the mounds of newsprint
and tangled strands of celluloid
these images are a hill too far.
What Lord Kitchener urged us to stop
is there before our eyes – a German soldier
raping a nun or is it one of ours
in a plundered uniform? One of those
unthinkables the sketches invite us to think.

'Very thorough people, the Germans,'
my grandfather told me
and we both knew what he meant.
Not the musicians. Not the artists.
Not the younger generations
whom Granddad would never know.
No doubt he meant the people
who numbered Dix among
the degenerate artists of Weimar
for Dix a badge of honour
that matched his Iron Cross.

A walk-through of Anish Kapoor

(Museum of Contemporary Art: Sydney 2013)

As I pace past the stainless steel surfaces
of the 'S Curve', my two hydrocephalic heads
melt and merge into each other, then lose themselves
in my spreading shoulders. I start to burrow
into familiar phrases: 'I felt the ground shift
under my feet' 'this is how it looks from where I stand'
and think how easily the world slips its libretto,
is knocked sideways by illness or trickery with optics.
I search for words to frame the philosophical
question the brochure invites me to ask: how the self
can curdle, separate or drain away into
the gaze of others, how its singularity
can be taken for granted by no one else
who doesn't have a privileged sense of its history.

At 'My Red Homeland' I see tons of wax
the colour of clotting blood, worried at clock-speed
by a motorised half-caliper, tipped with a steel
cube the size of a small container on a ship's deck.
I have a stomach that thinks like a stomach, easily
unsettled by a crushing weight of stimulus.
The robotic march of metal through soft matter
evokes the slow-motion, stylised violence
of films that ask me to reach back through artifice
and distancing to the roots of empathy, a swift sense
of being gutted by proxy. I try to guess how many
truckloads of visual metaphor it took to make this,
then baulk at shaping a philosophical question
too easy to pose and too hard to answer.

I look again at the circular creep of metal,
plough or military tank, through red earth ready
for seeding or the mud of battlefields, layers
of graveyards and vanished cities, a soil fertilised
by the dissolution of forgotten lives. I am now
in the actuarial zone where life starts to shrink
into the boutique theatre of kin and friends
where you chase memories uphill to a tipping point
of breathlessness before they start to chase you
with minds of their own. Your navel contemplation
is a way of logging in to the wheel of existence
where offcuts of information peel away like
the flecks and ribbons of red clay. It's all about
the journey, getting to nowhere elegantly, naked.

Horn

I look at Bernie McGann's saxophone
left on the stand in the break between sets
inert and unresolved like a question-mark
uncoupled from a very important question
and tumbled on its back all bumps and
corrugations like its owner's face and the same
ginger-snap colour with the sheen rubbed off
the bell gaping like a death mask   the greenish
tinge of a long wasting disease stealing
over its lips   waiting   like an old dog tied up
outside a pub for its master to shuffle out
and take it for a final lollop in the park
put it through its larrikin paces and old tricks.

Branford Marsalis: Concert in New Orleans

The notes hit the receptors and spread
sweet confusion, a multimedia event
beneath the grizzled canopy of my skull –
scum on a bayou surface and bubbles under,
fried catfish and tabasco freeing their scents
to frisk in the glades and thickets of my head.
Frets and stops and keys dance rainbows
that tell no stories beyond the chassé
of their own elegant acrobatics,
like the sift and winkle-pick of mathematics,
pure and sufficient only unto the day.
At the end of the set, applause like hailstones.

Jazz music recollected in tranquillity
is a contradiction or two in terms
or a hoop-snake that swallows itself whole,
from wheel to microdot as it stops rolling.

Hancock–Corea Concert

(Sydney Opera House, 1.6.15)

Two pianos, four hands, a single sheet of music
as an aide-memoire that they'd hardly need,
more a sight-gag to trigger some light banter
to reassure the listeners that they're only
mortals with clever fingers. Then off they go.
A recipe for randomness and incoherence
that isn't quite, tiptoeing through a trillion
possibilities on an invisible tightrope.

I've always wanted to google 'improvisation'
and slide into a bibliography, works
by musicians, brain specialists, philosophers.
I'm uneasy about mystique, hooked
on arrivals, in this case, regrettably,
silence. After the joy of getting there.

Improvisation

It's an algorithm that predigests the unexpected
and careers ahead of itself. It wouldn't happen
without memory that builds to overflow
before the first note then moves through
itself into something else, too fast to be
felt for what it is. At 8.5 eighth notes per
second, the spaces might have to be filled
with familiar runs and flurries from the
rehearsal room. Riffs climb on one another's
shoulders like storm-driven ruffles of surf.
A saxophone can spin into a high-speed crash
and concertina itself into massed chords.
It's as prime and risky a number as a one-line
stanza or a tightrope of eleven frayed strands.

Risk is a bridge between one orthodoxy and
the next, the exhilaration of getting there.
The programming set by thousands of hours
of practice is fallibly and unpredictably human,
enough to feel sick of itself and opt for novelty,
disguise and surprise, like a tennis smash
that props and feathers into a drop volley,
first because it can, then because it needs to.

It's an invitation to improvise a life,
walking away from what it was and where
it was heading, into something indeterminate
that can only stop but never finish, though
making it up as you go can wear you down.
There's a cracking point for the ill-prepared and
the under-rehearsed. Watch stoned musicians
and their stoned listeners rapt at the endless
formulaic noodling, the junk, the rubble.

You can seem to improvise on nothing but not
on a base of zero. There's an original score that
won't go away, starting and ending with a
retrospective. You're history, lit by dead stars,
beaming your own projections past rainbows
into black holes. Look back at your improvised
life and from the best angle, it might be
a one-night-only concert, all blurred rush
with a shimmer of post-coital afterglow.

After Bird

A butcher-bird sings punctually at six a.m.
dancing ribbons of melody, each line of ten notes
with a shorter bridge of four or five, then a reprise
after an irregular number of pulse beats.
The song seems to link arms with a tune by a young
Ornette Coleman: little mariachi licks, slurred runs
in the lower register, honks and sudden fractures
with blue notes and field cries tipping into the crevices.

It's an early spring so perhaps there are two of them,
long lines from the male bird, answers from the female
or vice versa, since no one else speaks butcher-bird
fluently, no more than anyone else, it seemed to me
at the time, could respond to Ornette Coleman,
discovered like first love and hugged to the breast
as a code open to no one else, tapped out
in ragged bursts with a hesitant grasp of sequence
at an age when commitment to a given direction
seemed to close off all other possibilities.

One butcher-bird, or even two, doesn't freshen
an old metaphor but he times his arrival perfectly,
in tune with an old prostate and an old brain
grateful for the small mercy of waking.
Ornette, when last I heard, was still playing
and hailed as an elder statesman of jazz.
We are borne back ceaselessly into new beginnings,
a thread of narrative, a few bars of the song.

Dream Homes

In my dreams I have often tapped into
the false memory of homes I have never lived in
slapped together from a kit of architectural
and narrative clichés: a harbourside flatette
with no definable features but outside stairs
and a dresser filled with unsecured secrets;
a spacious open-plan apartment with an
indoor garden tended by unseen hands;
a two-storey terrace with upstairs rooms
which were never used, lounges and libraries
with not a bedroom in sight. And none
of these homes was a primary residence,
all bolt-holes to escape to, safe houses
to hide the residue of unnamed crimes,
places to bring an unsuitable lover to
or work on the draft of an explosive memoir.

A diet of crime and espionage fiction might
explain the building blocks but not the impulse.
An analyst might look for an unhappy child
with a self that fitted badly which he needed
a weekend retreat away from. The social realist
might posit something sterner and more mundane:
A North Shore Sydney boy obsessed with
real estate options? Who would have thought?

Perhaps it's just a random playing-out of our
common condition: 'homo somnifaciens'
who needs doors opening onto other lives
and possibilities, or a transfer station for psychic
waste and old embarrassments. Dream homes
might be a free translation of the well-known
dream of flying, clear of that other dream
of a long corridor that debouches into another day
or not, like a bird dreaming of not flying.

The Third Man

I have been reading a book review of a new biography
of Proust, written in love for the subject and respect
for the author, with a sharp but delicate candour
in sentences beautifully shaped and sustained.
To do otherwise would jar, I suppose, like an oxymoron.
He discusses Proust's own view of the shaky parameters
of biography, written or caught in flight by the psyche
in a world of social pretensions and loose gossip,
till chronology melts on the page and I'm listening
to the three of them in warm and courteous debate.

The thought of an afterlife as the starting point of civilised
conversations must have soothed the pain of Proust's labours.
A trivial milieu was all he had to work with and if not, what?
He had never trained for anything else. Now we are four.

Henry and Margaret

In my grandmother's attic, photos of her own
parents that seem to have stories to tell:

What can go wrong at a wedding in 1903?
Nerves and second thoughts. Nothing has changed.
The boozy uncle. Don't keep topping him up.
The flirty cousin who aims herself at puddles
for a chance to lift her skirts and show her ankles.
The ghost of the first dress you almost ordered
come back to haunt you. The rehearsal:
fluffed lines and fumbling with rings. Thoughts
of the first night, for which there was no rehearsal.
Deep breath, fingers crossed and count to ten.
It will all be perfect. In hindsight, better than that.

Katoomba, September 24th. Dinner at the Carrington.
A newspaper picked from the rack at the desk.
A new prime minister. Deakin. 'A sound fellow,'
says Henry. 'Trust a man with a sucked-in belly
and a trimmed beard.' Now the newly-weds are
watching shadows sweep across the Jamieson Valley.
The merest touch of fingers as the menu is passed
from Margaret to Henry, contained and proper
but with a flare of intimacy, like Cubans dancing
the habanera, straight-backed but seeming to
step their way over a bed of molten lava.

Did their passion survive the loss of a child,
the chronic illness of another, jobs he sometimes
hated but couldn't do without? I like to think it did,
from the warmth that kept its glow as they aged in
the photos, a sense that the sum of them was more
than the parts. In the last photo, Henry, now in a
home for the bewildered, stares at a button on his coat
and whispers, 'I've seen one of those before. I think
it goes with something.' Margaret explains softly
as she folds him gently in her arms and rocks him.

Guard Duty

This side of my eyelids is a dark that lacks
density, matt patches of light tempering
the spread of shadow, wrinkles of glass-shatter

frozen just short of a drop, a millimetre
of airy perspective with a hint of
comic-book stars that follow a knock-out punch

or the thirty-six candles of the French
translation from the graphic, a black and white
negative of the New Year pyrotechnics,

son et lumière, fridge-hum and a faint spill
of streetlight. *Bonne année* indeed, bonnier
than the last one or the one before, if I lived

my life backwards or were legally blind
to all the evidence. I wait for sleep to shut
the world off like a falconer's hood.

The composer turns to the camera

windows of a soul well schooled
in nuance and discrimination.
He wears the cravat, vest
and shark-fin lapels of his age
and class. The white beard,
combed and fluffed, half hides
lips that promise to gather
into a faint moue of diffidence
in the face of this clapping
contraption and its hooded keeper.
'They think,' he thinks, 'to capture
an Age on the wing, like netting
a butterfly. But I know better.
Exegi monumentum perennius aere.
A man who knew about brass
and woodwinds and the strings
of Orpheus, music to buzz
in the ears of a thousand
generations. *Voilà*.'
Done. A minor inconvenience
quickly forgotten.

His music more slowly forgotten
but fading, the name already
with the whiff of a footnote about it.
He is teetering, like Blondin,
over the Niagara of oblivion.
His best-loved work is a pastorale,
composed behind closed shutters
to block out the *mugissements*
of the marching Prussians, the cries
of the Communards up against the walls
of the Père Lachaise. The people who praised

his stubborn devotion to his art
have gone to their graves or chosen
silence. *La petite phrase de Vinteuil,*
a fictional composer invented
by his younger and socially invisible
contemporary, Marcel Quelconque,
is unhummable but better known.

What is easiest forgotten
is why any of this might be remembered,
less lasting than bronze plaques
or original scores preserved under glass.
With empyrean calm, the composer
sits comfortably now with his own minority.
His modest ranking on the zeitgeist index
means nothing in eternity. He watches
the mortals left behind, clinging to drifting
data like shipwrecked sailors, within their grasp
all of history and none of it.

Radical Dementia

When I'm stressed I get completely beside myself
to my left in fact where there isn't all that much room
so we both sweat in the skin-crawling certainty
that right-thinking people are meaning to harm us
and have doubled us out for special treatment
by activating the tiny implants in our brains
that tell us to climb safety fences and take to the air
then we unstop the medication before it's too late
a holistic solution which makes me calm as a lake
cupped by mountains and holding its breath then
counting to ten then counting backwards in fifty
dialects of babel then sleeping for a day and a half
till the waking breeze starts humming the same song
and we both know where we stand and for how long.

Post Truth

There's a ban in downtown Pyongyang
on the public possession of onions
designed for performance enhancement

in the non-spontaneous displays of grief
that are mandatory at State Funerals.
Street-market-savvy sniffer dogs

slalom through the throng in the Square
barking at carry bags and handkerchiefs
and following through with sharp attacks

on sensitive parts of the body. Sources
close to the White House have whispered
that such procedures may be used to monitor

mourners at a putative memorial service
if ever Navy Seals in white coats whisk
their leader away for a session of triage

in the loading bay at Bellevue, thence to a
place whence no traveller ever returns, a coup
dear to the heart of hardcore Obamists.

This may be a fake news item bombing
us from Montenegro or Fox News or it
just might be a double bluff. Trust no one.

Navigation

A blind woman is being taught to use a cane
by a carer taught to conjure up total darkness
and translate it into imagined geometry.

She's newly blind perhaps through illness or mishap
or having crossed a line from partial sight
to the status of object, mere displacement of air.

Is the street completely unfamiliar or newly so,
turned into a slalom course of jostle and shin-bark,
or a field of unknown depth that needs sounding?

For a sighted person, it is like trying to remember
a child's unnameable world of unknowing.
You can shut your eyes in a parody of empathy

knowing you can open them on what was there before
and feel ashamed of taking for granted
a fragile, fallible thing, so easily tricked

by a magician's patter and business. You look
at the buildings opposite, a forest of shapes:
torches, wafer biscuits, giant cellphones,

all standing on end, with a gap in the middle,
half-obscured, that has to be guessed at:
a crater hollowed out by a meteorite, more

predictably, an excavation for underground
parking, a grassed space, a squat old building
saved and cocooned in new surroundings.

You have a context to guess from. For the blind,
the visual context is zero, data from the other
senses, but otherwise, all gap and conjecture.

Out of the corner of your eye that is spreading,
your optometrist warns, slowly and inexorably
towards the other corner, are the blurred shapes

of the carer and the blind woman who have edged
their way to a point between you and your bus stop.
You skirt around them, aiming a nod and a smile

at the carer, then, inexplicably, at the blind woman,
as if a smile could send vibrations through the air,
perceptible to a sixth sense called in to replace

the one lost, or perhaps just a wasted gesture
of fellow feeling, drifting off into the dark
for the pure relief and pleasure of the giver.

Panguna

Leavings from a mine on Bougainville,
a pool of slurry with a rainbow tinge on top
transmogrified into Art Doco at the Gallery.
The face of the local woman sifting and stirring
has the depth and texture of a map of sorrow.
The mine was a pot of gold to offshore stakeholders
till it went belly up, the jobs jobs jobs they promised,
nothing but a dirty trickle of royalties, then a past
and future that had lost all meaning. Thousands
of dead in the name of budget repair to the opaque
personal accounts of kleptocrats and the pale
myth of the sturdy integrity of a nation-state.
We could learn from this but haven't and won't,
about land loyally tenanted but never owned.

Unravelling

My dream has a twilight clarity, focus
and definition with a dominant image:
a cockatoo of an incandescent white,
screaming with paradoxical softness,
rubs noses with a cat of the same colour
but more muted, taking its light from within,
not from the setting sun or the rising moon.
It must be the Garden of Eden or somewhere
close by, perhaps Merimbula. The tribes
have come back, still watchful but more
at ease. Ben Boyd has issued a gruff
apology to man and beast and grows
sweet potatoes and bean shoots. I'm seven
years old again and my back doesn't hurt.

Blurb and Counter-blurb

'The poems are offline and heterodox
but the poet is crazy like a fox.'
– Alex Pope Jnr, Director of Creative Writing,
Prairie College, Nebraska

'Master of arity and nullary unions.
Commands the spaces left by the slippage
between the precognitive and the manifest.'
– Con Djinnshallah, Visiting Poet Fellow,
Spooner House, Oxford

'There is an unearned quality about his originality,
as if he is always writing a pastiche
of some work of which he has the only copy.
You remember nothing from his scribblings
except the curious way he goes about them.'
– Zelko Boz, Psychotherapist, Zagreb

'As topical as a new book on Roger Casement –
daft puns, a recycled smoking-room yarn.
It's a bit like Cabaret Night in the basement
of the British Embassy in Teheran.'
– Roger deCoverly-Larkin, Foreign Service (retired)

www.ingramcontent.com/pod-product-compliance
Lightning Source LLC
Chambersburg PA
CBHW070938080526
44589CB00013B/1551